Merman in My Tub 6

ORENCHI NO FURO JIJO

story & art by
ITOKICHI

KASUMI

Tatsumi's little sister. Loves her big brother very much. Her rival is Wakasa.

TATSUMI

The owner of the house. High school boy. He's good at cooking and household chores.

HISATORA UNCLE

Tatsumi's uncle. He develops suspicious medicines and has Tatsumi test them out.

SOUSUKE

Tatsumi's friend. He has two older sisters.

MAKI

A snail that appears quietly at the bath. Super near-sighted and has a negative personality.

WAKASA

The free-loading fish of the house. His age... don't ask.

MIKUNI

A jellyfish that wanders into the bath. His body is 99% water. He loves Aquarius.

AGARI

A shark that suddenly appears in the bath. It seems he is Wakasa's senpai.

TAKASU

An octopus that sometimes appears in the bath. Seems to be long-time friends with Wakasa. He's good at massages.

ECHIZEN

A super-sadistic crab that suddenly appeared. He is trying to take Wakasa back to the water.

GOROMARU

A starfish that appears in the house and often goes unnoticed. He is skilled at clinging.

SEVEN SEAS ENTERTAINMENT PRESENTS

Merman in My Tub

story and art by ITOKICHI   volume 6

TRANSLATION
Angela Liu

ADAPTATION
T Campbell

LETTERING
Laura Scoville

LOGO DESIGN
Meaghan Tucker

COVER DESIGN
Nicky Lim

PROOFREADER
Patrick King
Danielle King

ASSISTANT EDITOR
Jenn Grunigen

PRODUCTION ASSISTANT
CK Russell

PRODUCTION MANAGER
Lissa Pattillo

EDITOR-IN-CHIEF
Adam Arnold

PUBLISHER
Jason DeAngelis

MERMAN IN MY TUB VOL. 6
© Itokichi 2015
First published in Japan in 2015 by KADOKAWA CORPORATION, Tokyo.
English translation rights reserved by Seven Seas Entertainment, LLC.
under the license from KADOKAWA CORPORATION, Tokyo.

Seven Seas books may be purchased in bulk for promotional, educational, or business use. Please contact your local bookseller or the Macmillan Corporate and Premium Sales Department at 1-800-221-7945, extension 5442, or by e-mail at MacmillanSpecialMarkets@macmillan.com.

Seven Seas and the Seven Seas logo are trademarks of Seven Seas Entertainment, LLC. All rights reserved.

ISBN: 978-1-626924-36-9

Printed in Canada

First Printing: March 2017

10 9 8 7 6 5 4 3 2 1

FOLLOW US ONLINE: www.gomanga.com

READING DIRECTIONS

This book reads from *right to left*, Japanese style. If this is your first time reading manga, you start reading from the top right panel on each page and take it from there. If you get lost, just follow the numbered diagram here. It may seem backwards at first, but you'll get the hang of it! Have fun!!

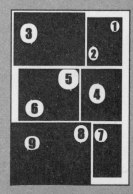

THE BEST COORDINATION

KNIT X DENIM

WHAT DOES THIS MEAN?!

HUH?

WHAT IS IT?!

. . . .

KNIT X DENIM

STARE

HM?

HEY. HEY. TAKE A LOOK AT THIS.

SPLISH!

FOR SOME REASON, I COULDN'T BRING THIS UP UNTIL NOW, BUT...

CHAPTER **73**

LET'S STUDY!!

WHY WOULD A MERMAN KNOW ABOUT TIMES?! I DON'T HAVE A WATCH!

HE'S GETTING DEFENSIVE!

LIKE I SAID! THIS "X" MARK RIGHT HERE!! WHAT IS IT?!

WHAT DO YOU MEAN?

POINT POINT

SPLISH SPLISH

NO WAY!

WELL, YOU'RE RIGHT.

THERE'S NO REASON FOR A MERMAN TO DO MULTIPLICATION TABLES.

I SEE THE DISBELIEF ON YOUR FACE THAT I'VE BEEN READING MAGAZINES WITHOUT KNOWING!!

I NORMALLY KEEP GOING AFTER GETTING THE GENERAL IDEA OF WHAT IT WAS TRYING TO SAY!!

. . . . .

I SEE... WHAT DOES IT MEAN?

NO, NO. SORRY. THAT'S A "TIMES" SIGN.

. . . . .

WITHOUT TAX.

HOW MUCH WOULD THREE MAGAZINES COSTING 500 YEN BE IN TOTAL?

I DON'T KNOW WHAT I DON'T KNOW!!!

ビ゛ DA-DAAAN

500円 × 3 BOOKS = 1500円

SO YOU USE IT LIKE THAT.

I SEE!!

HMM?

ONE TIMES TWO IS TWO?

ONE TIMES ONE IS ONE.

WHY DO I HAVE TO CHANGE, TOO?

HE AT LEAST LOOKS THE PART.

LET'S START WITH THE TIMES TABLE.

I'M A WHAT!?

I'M A LITTLE WORRIED HE'LL MISUSE THIS.

ARE YOU GOING TO BE ALL RIGHT?

EVEN THOUGH HE'S A MERMAN, HE LOOKS LIKE AN ADULT.

THOUGH, IT TAKES ON A DIFFERENT MEANING WHEN IT'S USED LIKE THAT IN A MAGAZINE.

SIX TIMES SEVEN IS FORTY-TWO.

SIX TIMES EIGHT IS FORTY-EIGHT...

WAKASA.

I SHOULD TEACH HIM A LITTLE. WHETHER HE USES IT OR NOT IS UP TO HIM, SAME AS IT IS FOR ANYBODY ELSE.

NO, FORTY-EIGHT. SIX TIMES NINE...

THA-THUMP...!

FERDIE ATE...?! WHAT'D FERDIE EAT?

I WOULD LIKE TO STUDY, TEACHER!!

EVEN KASUMI KNOWS HOW TO MULTIPLY.

MEN WITH BAD MATH BRAINS AREN'T POPULAR.

One hour later.

TATSUMI, I MEMORIZED THEM ALL~!

THERE WERE SO MANY...

SHAKE

SHAKE

Multiplication Table

REALLY?

THEN, LET ME TEST YOU.

PUSH

GLEAM

7 × 6?

42!

↑
An upper-level question that's easy to get wrong.

AH HA HA...

FU FU FU...

HE'S GOOD ...!!

OKAY!!

FLAP FLAP

I'LL LEAVE YOU BEHIND IF YOU CAN'T KEEP UP!!

MORE IMPORTANTLY, HE MEMORIZED THEM SO QUICKLY...!!

PLEASE DON'T TALK DURING CLASS.

TEACHER, MY NOTEBOOK PRUNED UP!!

Japanese.

PRUNE

I SEE... HE'S STILL A CHILD ON THE INSIDE.

GASP!!

DAZE

IN OTHER WORDS, HE'S STILL LIKE A SPONGE FOR KNOWLEDGE...!!

DRY

FLIP FLIP FLIP
ペラ ペラ ペラ

History.

I SEE... SO *THAT'S* WHY THE SEA WAS SO NOISY THEN.

BLACK SHIPS?

WHAT IS THIS BOOK?

RISE

WAKASA.

THIS IS THE CONTAINER YOUR UNCLE'S BATH SALTS ARE ALWAYS IN!

OH! THIS!

SPLISH

Sci...

SPLISH

Commodore Perry Matthew arrived in Japan

I'M ALWAYS SERIOUS.

You can't help wanting to let a sponge soak up water.

WANT TO TRY AND TAKE THIS SERIOUSLY?

THUD THUD THUD

Science
Physical Education
Chemistry
Mathematics
Rakugo
Arithmetic
Science
Japanese

YES, TEACHER!

ASK ME IF YOU HAVE ANY QUESTIONS.

SRTCH SRTCH SRTCH SRTCH

YEAH.

I CAN... I CAN REALLY DO THIS!!

HERE. YOU DO THIS.

I SEE. I SEE.

PUFF PUFF

HE STICKS TO THINGS LONGER IF HE HAS AN ULTERIOR MOTIVE.

HE'S MORE MOTIVATED THAN USUAL.

I THINK MAYBE WE CAN USE THESE DRILLS.

I'M SURE EVERYONE WILL BE SURPRISED WHEN THEY SEE ME LOOKING LIKE A PROFESSOR.

FU FU...

For a second...

he comes back to himself, and wonders why he's getting so serious about this.→

· · · ·

HEY HEY HOH...

Naked.
↓

SCRIBBLE SCRIBBLE SCRIBBLE

A PROFESSOR?

YEAH.

BUT, WELL, YOU KNOW.

MOOOAN

Glucose for the Brain (Cocoa)
↓

WE MADE YOUR BRAIN WORK TOO HARD.

I'M STARTING TO GET DIZZY.

HM?

AOOON

TA...

TATSU-MI...

ALL I SEE ARE LETTERS IN FRONT OF ME.

I'M...

HAVING A LOT OF FUN.

THERE WASN'T ANYONE TO TEACH ME UNTIL NOW.

WAKASA.

SPARTAN!!

WHAT ARE YOU RESTING FOR?

MOVE YOUR HANDS.

HE STUDIED LATE INTO THE NIGHT.

WAKE UP.

WAKASA.

SHAKE

WAKASA.

SCRATCH

TA...

TATSU-MI...!

SCRATCH

WE'RE GOING TO CONTINUE FROM YESTERDAY.

ONE... ONE TIMES ONE...

TIME FOR BREAKFAST BUNS...

WHAT WAS THAT AGAIN?

IT'S LOOPING IN MY HEAD...!!

The water-soaked sponge...

Has dried out overnight.

IT'S MORNING AND I'M ALREADY SO HUNGRY...

GROOWL

PA-CHINK

I'LL GO MAKE BREAKFAST.

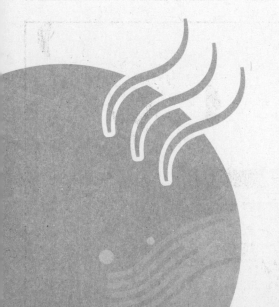

オレん家のフロ事情

GOODNESS! DON'T SAY SUCH MEAN THINGS~!

......

I'LL HEAD TO BED AFTER WATCHING THIS!

YEAH!

SEE YOU LATER. DON'T STAY UP TOO LATE.

GOOD NIGHT!

GLANCE

......

WHO SAID THAT?

GLANCE

BEEP

I WILL NOT ADD MORE HOT WATER.

HM HM HMMM~

CHAPTER 74

KYUU-CHAN THE WATER HEATER

TH-TH-
THE WATER
HEATER
SP...

S P O K E...!!

IT'S
THE
MIDDLE
OF THE
NIGHT.
BE
QUIET.

WHAT
ARE
YOU
MAKING
A
RUCKUS
FOR?

"WHO
SAID
THAT?"
WHAT A
LAME
RE-
SPONSE.

DON'T
LOOK AT
ME WITH
PITYING
EYES!!

I
SEE.

. . . . . .

?

WHAT?!
THIS
THING IS
TALKING
?!!

WAAAAAH?!

SPLISH SPLISH

EVERY DAY,
YOU PUSH ME
THERE AND
FORCE ME TO
SPOUT HOT
LIQUID FOR
YOU—

YOU
ALWAYS
PUSH
DOWN ON
MY RED
PART
WITHOUT
HESITATION.

SEE
!!

IT
SPEAKS
WHEN I
PUSH IT
HERE!!

BEEP

I'M
NOT
LYING!!

IF
YOU'RE
GOING
TO LIE,
MAKE
UP A
BETTER
LIE.

SPLISH SPLISH SPLISH

I
CAN'T
BELIEVE
YOU DID
SOME-
THING
LIKE THAT
WHILE I'M
SO
HELP-
LESS...

YOU'RE
MISUNDER-
STANDING
!!

WAAAH
!!

OVER
AND
OVER
AGAIN,
SO
RELENT-
LESSLY
...

ADDING
ADDITIONAL
HOT
WATER.

THIS
ISN'T
HOW IT
LOOKS
!!

FLINCH

GA-CHAK

WA-
KASA!

YEAH, YOU'RE RIGHT.

IT REALLY SPOKE.

CLENCH

WHAT'S WRONG?! WHY ARE YOU STAYING QUIET?!

HUH ?!

SMACK

SMACK

I'M TELLING THE TRUTH~!

SOB

SOB

SOB

KA-CHUNK

LYING IS BAD, WAKA-SA.

IF YOU CAUSE A RUCKUS IN THE MIDDLE OF THE NIGHT AGAIN, NO AFTERNOON SNACK.

NO WAY!!

SEE--?!!

COME BACK, TATSUMI!!!

IN YOUR FACE.

RIGHT.

CAREFULLY

Zzzz

I'M NOT A HARD **OBJECT** LIKE YOU!

YOU DON'T HAVE TO RUN.

WE'RE A LOT ALIKE.

FLINCH

IT'S POINT-LESS TRYING TO SHUT ME OFF.

YOU JUST CALLED ME A MON-STER...!!

BUT YOU ARE A MONS... UM, I MEAN...

YOU'RE UNIQUE.

I AM THE WATER HEATER OF THIS HOUSE.

SOB

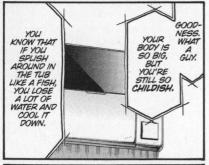

YOU KNOW THAT IF YOU SPLISH AROUND IN THE TUB LIKE A FISH, YOU LOSE A LOT OF WATER AND COOL IT DOWN.

YOUR BODY IS SO BIG, BUT YOU'RE STILL SO CHILDISH.

GOOD-NESS, WHAT A GUY.

Objects used by humans for a long time can sometimes be imbued with such a spirit.

COULD IT BE YOU'RE A TSUKU-MOGAMI...?!

WHILE THE OWNER HAS CHANGED, THE HEART OF THIS HOUSE LIVES ON.

GUH. I'M SORRY...

PRICK

AND SOME-TIMES YOUR FIN HURTS.

WHY DON'T YOU HAVE ANY RE-STRAINT?

I SEE YOU DO THIS EVERY DAY.

YOU WHACK ME WITH IT.

PRICK

PRICK

I'M SORRY... MA'AM?

I...

PRICK

FROM THE SUDDEN INCREASE OF USE I'VE HAD LATELY, I'VE GOTTEN OLD QUITE FAST.

It seems that the water heater is sensitive about her age.

PLISH...

PRICK

AHHH...

TATSUMI-SAMA TOUCH-ED MY BUTTON...!!

UGH...

WHY... DO I KEEP GETTING INTO TROUBLE...?

OH, HOW LONG IT HAS BEEN...?!

I FEEL SOME-HOW... LIKE I'M GETTING YELLED AT BY TATSU-MI...

YOU GUYS SAY THE SAME THINGS.

WHAT?

IF YOU LIKE HIM SO MUCH,

WHY ARE YOU STAYING QUIET?

......

BE-BEEP

88°C

I...

I'M LIKE TAT-SUMI-SAMA...?!

TAT-SUMI-SAMA?!

TATSUMI-SAMA IS MY MAS-TER.

A SERVANT LIKE ME SHOULDN'T CALL OUT TO HIM.

BUT I'M OKAY?

BEEP BEEP BEEP BEEP BEEP

YOU'RE OVER-FLOWING HOT WATER!!

CALM DOWN!!

BUT I CAN'T POSSI-BLY...!!

TH-TH-TH-THAT MAKES ME SO HAP-PY...

I'M NOT A PET!! I'M A FRIEND!!

YOU'RE JUST HIS PET, RIGHT?

SPLISH

SPLISH

GA-CHAK

WA-KASA!!

IT'S NOT ME!!

SILENCE...

WHEN HE WOULD ONLY TAKE BATHS WITH HIS GRAND-FATHER.

HEY, KYUU-CHAN.

WHO ARE YOU CALLING KYUU-CHAN?

ISN'T IT LONELY TO STAY HERE AND NEVER TALK TO TATSUMI?

WHEN HE ONCE ALMOST DROWNED IN THE TUB.

AND WHEN HE WAS ALONE...

YOU THINK SO?

SECRETLY PLAYING WITH DUCKY...

IN THE PAST, THERE WERE TIMES IT ONLY SEEMED APPRO- PRIATE.

AH-CHOO!

HEEEEK!

SO TRUE!

GIGGLE

GIGGLE

WOULD HE WANT TO KNOW THAT I HAD ALWAYS BEEN WATCHING?

THOSE ARE SPECIAL MEMO- RIES TO ME.

HUM...?

I FEEL LIKE I'VE BEEN TOLD THAT BEFORE...

YOU ARE A STRANGE ONE.

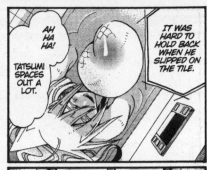

AH HA HA!

TATSUMI SPACES OUT A LOT.

IT WAS HARD TO HOLD BACK WHEN HE SLIPPED ON THE TILE.

UGH!

YOU'RE THE REASON TATSUMI-SAMA HATES TAKING A BATH.

BUT YOU ARE ALSO THE REASON HE TAKES BATHS MORE OFTEN NOW.

GASP!

I SHALL SHUT UP NOW.

I... I TALKED TOO MUCH ABOUT MY MASTER'S SECRETS.

WHY?!

RIGHT?!

THEN, KYUU-CHAN.

COME ON! DON'T HESITATE TO GET SPOILED BY ME.

I'M YOUR MASTER AS WELL!!

SINCE YOU CAN SPEAK...

YOU SHOULD TALK TO ME IF YOU CAN'T TALK TO TATSUMI!!

SO HOOOT!!

SPLISH

SPLISH

BLUB BLUB BLUB BLUB

YOU GET COCKY EASILY.

...!

SO COLD!!

WHY?!

25

HEY.

I DON'T HAVE HOT WATER OVER THERE.

HUH?

STOMP...

Next morning.

LAST NIGHT IT KEPT GETTING HOT AND COLD...

WHAT A TERRIBLE EXPERIENCE...

YAAAWN!

SLOSH

OUR HOT WATER ALL COMES FROM ONE TANK, SO I CAN TELL WHEN YOU OVERUSE IT.

KITCHEN   TANK   TUB

RUMBLE

SPLISH

RUMBLE

RUMBLE

HUH... WHAT ARE YOU...?

HMM?

HOW MUCH WATER DID YOU *USE UP* LAST NIGHT?

RUMBLE

IT... IT'S *NOT* MY FAULT ~!!

SAY SOMETHING, KYUU-CHAN ...!!!

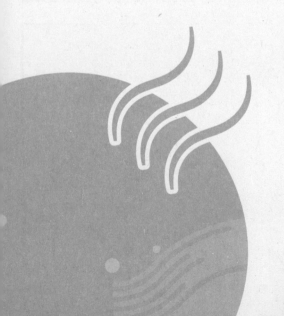

オレん家のフロ事情

GLIMMER

DO YOU HAVE BUSINESS WITH ME, HISA-TORA-SA--

BRR! SO COLD!

IT'S GREAT WEATHER FOR TAKING A BATH...

SHIVER

WAIT. WAIT. WAIT!

GRAB

SORRY, I MISTOOK YOU FOR SOMEONE ELSE.

I'M YOUR UNCLE!

FANCY SEEING YOU HERE!!

OOH ?!

IT'S TATSU-BOY!!

SOUNDS SO FAKE...

CHAPTER 75
TRUTH SERUM

SO, YOU DON'T HAVE A FIANCÉE YET.

CLOP CLOP CLOP CLOP

I'LL GET A WIFE THIS WAY!!

I'M SERIOUS THIS TIME!!

....

HAHAHA

I HOPE, ANYWAY! YOUR UNCLE FEELS REALLY LONELY!!

I'M GOING TO GET MARRIED SOON! ♡

WHY ARE YOU DRESSED SO FORMALLY?

USE THIS AND YOU'LL HAVE ONE.

PLOP

TEST THIS OUT ON SOME GIRLS AGAIN!

THERE IT IS.

HERE. ♡

SLOSH ♪

WELL, PUTTING ASIDE SMALL TALK.

GO MAKE SOME GIRLS FALL HEAD OVER HEELS FOR YOU!!

SEE YA!!

PLEASE DON'T GIVE ME ANYTHING THAT CAN EXPLODE.

HM? IT'S NORMAL.

WHAT IS IT THIS TIME?

ALL ALONE

SEE YA.

"NO... ALREADY. ♡ I'M GOING TO OVERFLOW. ♡" BATH SALT NUMBER 13.

DID YOU POUR IT IN ALREADY?

HE WASN'T PAYING ATTENTION AT ALL!!

LOOK AT ME, TATSUMI.

H...

HEY, WAIT...

SPLISH... SPLISH...

ビダビダビダビダ
SPLISH SPLISH SPLISH SPLISH

TA-DAA

!

HE'S CONFIDENT ABOUT THIS ONE.

AND SO HERE'S ANOTHER ONE.

ANOTHER ONE!!

HOW MANY CHEMICALS HAVE I TESTED FOR HIM NOW?!

WHAT KIND OF USE WOULD A CLUMSY AND SPACED-OUT GUY LIKE YOU BE?

THIS VOICE.....!!

HA HA HA HA!!

EASY FOR YOU TO SAY!!

WELL, WELL. YOU'VE ALWAYS BEEN FINE IN THE END.

ガ
RATTLE

ラッ

ECHI-ZEN!!

GOODNESS. YOU REALLY MAKE ME LAUGH.

GLANCE

→ Wants to be praised just a bit.

ARE THESE TESTS EVEN USE-FUL...?

I CAN TOO BALANCE A BALL ON MY NOSE!

YOU'RE LIKE A BABY SEA LION WHO CAN'T BALANCE A BALL ON HIS NOSE.

FWIP
ずぃっ

I HAVE NO PLANS TO BE FRIENDLY.

I'M A PROUD LONER CRAB.

KONK

HOT MILK...

SIP

YOU NEVER VISIT WITH WAKASA'S OTHER FRIENDS, I NOTICE.

MIKUNI-SAN, AGARI-SAN...

SPWASH

SO...

LET'S END THIS TODAY.

TATSUMI IS SO STRONG...

SLAP

YOU SHOULDN'T POINT SCISSORS AT PEOPLE!

HE THOUGHT HIS LIFE WOULD END.

THUMP THUMP THUMP

WELL, MAYBE IT IS TIME YOU MOVED ON. IF HE'LL HELP YOU, I'M COOL WITH IT.

YOU SHOULD BE FIGHTING FOR ME!!!

TATSU-MI!!

SURELY IT'S TIME TO END THIS SHAMEFUL DOMESTI-CATION?

PULL

BEING CARED FOR LIKE A PET BY A HUMAN.

YOU.

WAH!

AH!

SO...

KUH ...!

I CAN'T LET OUR SERIES END SO ABRUPTLY ...!!

BUT ECHIZEN'S STRONG ENOUGH TO TAKE ME IF HE WANTS.

GRAB

WAKA-SA...

GASP!

TATSU-MI!

TA-TATSU-MI!

SPLASH

DO SOME-THING, BATH SALTS !!!

WHERE THE TRUE MOTHER WAS THE ONE WHO WOULDN'T LET HER BABY BE TORN IN TWO...!!

IS THIS LIKE THE MOTHERS SOLOMON HAD TO JUDGE?!

NO, MINE!

THIS IS MY CHILD!

SILENCE...

SCRATCH

STARE

AHH~! WHICH HAND SHOULD I TAKE?

SCRATCH

THE CHAINS WERE OUTSIDE.

LET ME START OVER!

YOU HAVE CHAINS WITH YOU?!

OOPS, I FORGOT.

CHAINS?!

SHWUP

NOTHING HAPPENED

―?!

WHYYYYYY

...?!

NOW I'VE COME TO PICK YOU UP!!

WHY ARE YOU ACTING LIKE YOU JUST GOT HERE?!

THANKS FOR WAITING!!

JANGLE

ガッ RATTLE ラッ

HEEK

THAT'S THE WAY OF THE WORLD.

ECHIZEN SOUNDS STRANGE!!!

I HATE SALTS! I HATE THEM. BUT A LITTLE PART OF ME LOVES THEM.

YOU REALLY WANTED TO TEST THEM OUT.

ガッ ラッ
RATTLE

IT'S PRETTY COLD OUT THERE TODAY―

HEY.

ECHIZEN, ARE YOU STILL PLANNING ON TAKING ME BACK?

GONK

GUAH!

HEGH!

EVEN IF I HAVE TO CHAIN YOU DOWN.

YEAH.

オレん家のフロ事情

SHA-KING!!

SQUIRM!!

......

IT'S LIKE WATCHING A MONSTER FILM.

From the previous chapter.

These two are fighting (they don't get along).

CHAPTER **76**
TACCHAN AND ECCHAN

NICE CROSS-COUNTER...

RIGHT BACK AT YOU.

HMPH!

TCH!

WHY IS THIS GUY HERE?

HEH!

BUT IT LOOKS LIKE YOU'VE SETTLED IN PRETTY WELL IN A TUB LIKE THIS. IT SUITS YA.

TWITCH TWITCH

IF I KNEW AN OCTOPUS LIKE YOU WAS COMING...

THERE'S NO WAY I'D COME TO A TUB LIKE THIS.

TWITCH

EVEN TATSUMI IS GETTING ANGRY!!

WHAT CAN ONE FISH LIKE ME DO?!

HEEEK!

ゴ!! ゴ!! RUMBLE! RUMBLE!

WHAT DID YOU SAY...?

I CAN'T LET THAT SLIDE.

ゴ!! ゴ!! RUMBLE! RUMBLE!

THIS AND THAT ABOUT THE TUB.

Some Years Ago.

WH... WHAT'S GOING ON...?!

I.... I DON'T REALLY THINK THAT AT ALL!!

WHAT THE HELL?! THE WORDS CAME OUT OF MY MOUTH ON THEIR OWN!!

HM...

. . . . .

MY UNCLE WAS CONFIDENT WITH THESE "OVERFLOWING" BATH SALTS, SO I THINK THEY'RE MAKING YOU GUYS OVERFLOW.

WITH YOUR TRUE FEELINGS.

IT'S PROBABLY THE BATH SALTS.

GOODNESS!

EMPTY

YOU'RE IMAGINING THINGS.

NO, NOTHING.

WHAT DID YOU SAY...?

J... JUST NOW.

THIS IS A GOOD CHANCE.

ISN'T IT, WAKASA?

YOU'RE RIGHT, TATSUMI.

I WOULD HAVE SHOWN YOU THE RESULTS OF MY HARD SWIMMING TRAINING.

I WANT TO DO SEABED SOCCER AGAIN--

BOTH OF YOU SHOULD LET IT ALL FLOW~! ☆

NOW, LET IT ALL OUT!!

SNIP SNIP WIGGLE WIGGLE STOP IT!!

WAIT!

RATTLE RATTLE

. . . . .

AND THE "BABY" DIDN'T REALIZE IT.

HUH?! THAT'S WHAT IT WAS?!

FWIP

FWIP

YOU'RE PLAYING WITH HIM TOO MUCH!!

DON'T BLUSH LIKE THAT. DON'T.

IT WAS MY FAULT...?

WHAT SHOULD I DO, TATSUMI...

YOU'RE THE ONE WHO NEEDS TO BACK OFF!! MY TIME ISN'T FREE.

A CLOWN AND A PLAYBOY OF AN OCTOPUS.

AN UNLIKABLE BASTARD CRAB.

SO.

WHAT DO YOU THINK OF EACH OTHER?

SPLOSH

SPLOSH

UGH

CH

CH

CH

CH

CH

CH!!

HEY...

IT HURTS WHEN YOU PULL ME LIKE THAT-

I WANT TO PLAY WITH TACCHAN AGAIN.

I WANT TO MAKE UP WITH ECCHAN.

YOUR TRUE FEELINGS?

......

SLOP

A REAL SOLOMON TRIAL.

BUT THE ENDING WAS DIFFER- ENT.

SCREW YOU!!

HMPH.

I STILL REMEMBER IT SO CLEARLY.

......

BLUUUUSH

YOU'RE ONE HUNDRED YEARS TOO LATE, HUMAN CHILD!!

TRYING TO DEFEAT ME WITH YOUR MAGIC TRICKS!

WHAM

THESE ARE ALL LIES!!!

FORGET IT! FORGET IT!!

RAGH!

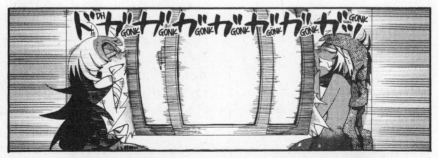

DH GONK GONK GONK GONK GONK GONK

THEY'RE COMPLETELY IN SYNC.

I'M GOING FIRST!!

I'M GOING TO LEAVE FIRST!!

WELL...

THEY NEED TIME.

SHAA

I WISH WE COULD ALL PLAY TOGETHER AGAIN.

NOW.

NO WAY.

COME OVER HERE, TATSUMI! ♡

DON'T YOU WANT TO EXPRESS TRUE FEELINGS?

NO. WAY.

SLOSH

RIGHT.

IT OVER-FLOWED!

OF COURSE IT WOULDN'T WORK ON YOU. YOUR FEELINGS ARE ALL ON THE SURFACE ANYWAY.

ALL THANKS TO THOSE BATH SALTS!

THOSE TWO BECAME HONEST WITH EACH OTHER--

SPLAAASH

Next Day.

SNIFF

I DIDN'T WANT TO HEAR WORDS LIKE "PERVERTED OLD MAN" AND "GROSS..."

UEH...

Sometimes the truth hurts.

I ACTUALLY THOUGHT... THERE'D BE AT LEAST ONE GIRL WHO'D LIKE ME.

UEH...

HIC!

オレん家のフロ事情

HUH?!

BUT I HAVE MY PART-TIME JOB, SO I CAN'T GO...

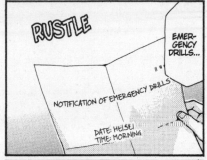

RUSTLE

EMERGENCY DRILLS...

NOTIFICATION OF EMERGENCY DRILLS

DATE: HEISEI
TIME: MORNING

BIG TALK FROM A GUY WHO CAN'T GET OUT OF THE TUB.

SPLASH SPLASH

YOU ALWAYS SEEM SO UNFOCUSED!!

WILL YOU BE ALL RIGHT, TATSUMI?!!

DRILLS TO CONFIRM WHEN TO EVACUATE AND HOW TO RESPOND DURING AN EMERGENCY.

EMERGENCY DRILLS? WHAT ARE THOSE?

OH! I SEE!

SO THAT'S WHAT IT IS!

CHAPTER 77

THE EMERGENCY DRILLS AT MY HOUSE

Rr Rr

HEY! HEY! HO!!

HO.

TATSU-MI!!

LET'S FIND A SOLUTION THAT LETS BOTH OF US SURVIVE IN ANY SITUATION!

A. TAKE HIM → WE WON'T MAKE IT OUT

B. LEAVE HIM → I LIVE, BUT HE DRIES UP AND DIES

THAT'S ABOUT IT. FOR YOU.

IF A GIANT'S SHAKING THE HOUSE AND A MERMAN'S IN THERE, I HAVE TWO OPTIONS.

TRUDGE

TRUDGE

Wet rice (for humidity). →

AND MOVE SLOWLY ALONG THE GROUND NEXT TO A WALL.

COVER YOUR HEAD WITH SOMETHING.

In case of earthquake.

SPLASH SPLASH SPLASH

LIKE WEIGHING DOWN THE HOUSE OR YOU GETTING STRONGER!!!

THERE'S NO WAY FOR BOTH OF US TO BE SAVED?!

HM?

DO WE NEED TO EAT DONUTS NOW?

OH, THANK GOODNESS. ♡

IT LOOKS LIKE THE BATHROOM AND BATH AREA ARE COMPARATIVELY SAFE.

WELL...

DONUTS

Don't push. Don't run. Don't talk.

......

↑ He means this!

SNAP

DONUTS...?

I WANT MINE HONEY-GLAZED, THEN!!

Has exploded in the past. ←

JUST END UP LIKE A REGULARLY-FRIED FISH...!

A FRIED FISH WITH LOTS OF OIL.

I'LL...

In case of fire.

WH- WHAT SHOULD I DO?!

SHIP ME OUT?!

WE'LL CHANGE IT TO: I WILL CARRY YOU AND SHIP YOU OUT.

STAY STILL LIKE A BRONZE STATUE.

I SHOULD TAKE NOTES.

MOST FIRES COME FROM THE KITCHEN STOVE.

SO WE HAVE A LOT OF TIME TO ESCAPE.

PONK PONK

DROOP

EVEN CARRIED I LOOK COOL AND MYSTERIOUS.

IT LOOKS LIKE YOU'D DRY UP REALLY QUICK.

WATER GUN!

THAT'S RIGHT, WAKASA.

DO YOU HAVE ANY SKILLS?

YOU'RE A MERMAN, RIGHT?

SPLITCH

I WISH YOU COULD EVOLVE, LIKE A POKÉMON.

SPLISH

SPLISH

S... SORRY. I'M A WATER-TYPE, BUT I'M JUST A MERMAN...

I CAN SPLASH AROUND...

PLAN A IS A NO GO.

HE'S BECOMING MORE OF AN... UNKNOWN CREATURE.

WIGGLE WIGGLE

SPLITCH

SPLITCH

OH! THIS IS PRETTY COOL LOOKING!!

· · · · · ·

DROOP...

BUT THIS IS ALL I HAVE...

THAT'S SURPRISINGLY LOGICAL OF YOU.

GASP!!

MY VALUABLES!!

I HAVE TO MAKE SURE WHAT TO BRING WITH ME WHEN THAT HAPPENS!!

IT CAN'T BE HELPED.

I'LL GIVE YOU THESE.

MATCH

!

THANK YOU!

HERE, TAKE THIS BAG FOR THEM.

DURING EMERGENCIES.

WE NEED CANDLES?

CLICK

CLICK

CLICK

BWOH

BWOH

WOW.

MAGAZINES, THE TV, DUCKY-CHAN...

WATER, A TOWEL, A FLASHLIGHT...

DON'T PLAY AROUND.

I LIT IT UP EASILY!!

EVEN I CAN DO IT!!

WOW!

ZIP

B-BUT THIS IS ALL I-HYA

TUUUUG

WE'RE NOT GOING ON A PICNIC, ARE WE?

OUR PREPARATIONS ARE PERFECT!!

RIGHT!!

GA-CHAK

IT'S DARK AND CROWDED IN TH--

YOU SHOULD STAY OUTSIDE, DUCKY-CHAN.

TONK

JEEZ, TATSUMI. PULL YOUR-SELF TOGETH-ER.

COME TO THINK OF IT, DID WE HAVE A FIRE EXTIN-GUISHER...?

HM? HUNH...

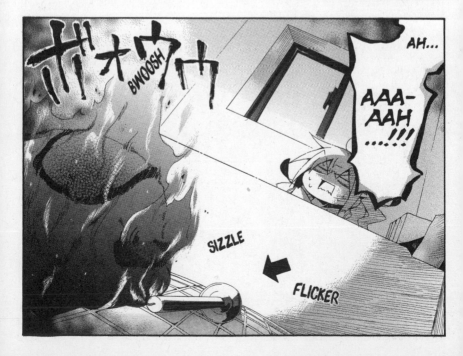

BWOOSH

AH...

AAA-AAH.....!!!

SIZZLE

FLICKER

Merman in My Tub

オレん家のフロ事情

HOLD ON A SEC-OND!!

I WORKED HARD TO MAKE THIS FOR MY BRO-THER!!

OH!

I WAS SAVING THAT FOR LAST~!

It is Christmas Eve.

GRAB GRAB GRAB

IT'S SO LIVELY.

MUNCH

I LOVE ALL OF KASUMI-DONO'S HANDMADE FOOD!!

MUNCH

CHAPTER 78

THE SANTA AT MY HOUSE

BIG BROTHER.

SNEAK

IT'S GOOD.

BIG BROTHER!! WHY DON'T THE TWO OF US CELEBRATE CHRISTMAS TOGETHER? ♡♡

BIG BROTHER!! LET US DO CHRISTMAS TOGETHER!!

TATSUMI!! LET'S DO CHRISTMAS!!

One Hour Earlier.

DA-DAAAN!!

HE BELIEVES IN SANTA!!

BING

I WOULD LIKE TO BORROW SOME SOCKS FOR THE NIGHT.

FREEZE

......

I WROTE HIM A LETTER ABOUT WHAT I WANTED.

EMBARRASSED

FOOD...

KASUMI-DONO...

INCH

INCH

I FORGOT ABOUT YOU, FISH-SAN...

Moment of Pause

TATSUMI IS GOING TO PLAY SANTA THIS YEAR, TOO...!

AS EXPECTED!!

BIG BROTHER, YOU KNOW A LOT!!

IT SEEMS THAT SHORT SOCKS ARE THE TREND NOWADAYS.

IT'S LIKE A KINDERGARTEN CHRISTMAS PARTY.

KYA KYA

CHATTER CHATTER

MY MEAT!

OKAY, NEXT PLATE.

SO DELICIOUS! MARRY ME!

YOU GUYS SHOULD BE A LITTLE MORE CONSIDERATE.

THEN YOU PREPARE AND LEAVE COOKIES AND MILK FOR HIM...

YOU PUT A LETTER IN A SOCK.

WHAT ARE YOU TALKING ABOUT?

WHAT ARE YOU DOING?

DO YOU NOT KNOW?

I'M WRITING TO SANTA.

SANTA'S NOT REAL.

YOU'RE SUCH A CHILD.

WHA...?!

C-CAN... YOU SAY WHAT HE'S LIKE...?

I WAS TOLD HE WAS!!

NO, HE ISN'T!!

HE'S REAL!!

HE- HE-

OH NO!

WHO TOLD YOU!!

GRAB

M.... MY, MY.

YOU DON'T KNOW?

REALLY, FISH-SAN?!

HM?

WA-KASA!!

HUUH?!

SMEAR

AND HE IS THE LEADER OF THE REINDEER THAT PULL THE SLED.

THERE IS A REINDEER WITH A RED NOSE NAMED RUDOLPH.

WELL...

GLANCE

UM...

GLANCE

OF...

HE'S GETTING INTO IT.

HE-HEEN!!

WITH THE COMPLETE TRUST OF SANTA, HE RUNS ACROSS THE STARRY NIGHT SKY!!

SPLISH

SPLISH

OOH!

NO WAY!!

SEE!!

The moment he became an adult.

OF COURSE HE'S REAL!!

R...

REINDEER ARE SMART AND STRONG.

THEY CAN DO ANYTHING!!

SOMETIMES HE EVEN RIDES DIRECTLY ON THE REINDEER TO GET THERE A LITTLE FASTER.

YES?

YES?

ON THAT SLED IS A MOUNTAIN OF PRESENTS...

AND THE KIND AND GENEROUS SANTA...

PUSH

PUSH

PUSH

IS THAT SO?

RIGHT ...

TATSUMI ?!

JERK PASSED IT ON TO ME!

SO SANTA REALLY IS REAL.

GLOW

Y... YEAH.

HE'S AN AMAZING OLD MAN WHO PASSES OUT PRESENTS TO KIDS THROUGHOUT THE WORLD.

I'M PRETTY SURE HE HAS A BEARD LIKE THIS.

They were able to protect the secret.

I'LL GIVE YOU THE OTHER HALF OF THE SOCKS!

YEAH.

I'LL WRITE A LETTER TO SANTA, TOO.

IT IS FINE!!

I'M SORRY, STARFISH-SAN.

YEAH.

OH, LATELY, IT SEEMS HE ENTERS THROUGH THE FRONT DOOR OF MANY HOUSES.

BUT THERE AREN'T ANY HOUSES WITH CHIMNEYS AROUND HERE.

I KNOW !!

HE ENTERS THROUGH THE CHIMNEY!!

IT'S ALL RIGHT.

I'M THE ONLY ONE LEFT OUT...!!

I WAS ABLE TO GET THE LETTERS.

TINGLE

TINGLE

WE WERE ABLE TO PROTECT THE DREAMS OF CHILDREN.

THANK GOODNESS...

KYAA

THOUGH, NOT WITHOUT COST TO OUR-SELVES.

KYAA

RUSTLE

I WONDER WHAT THEY WANT.

DEAR SANTA, I WOULD LIKE YOU TO COME THIS YEAR. I WANT MEAT THAT LOOKS LIKE IT DOES IN MANGA.

DEAR SANTA, THANK YOU FOR EVERY-THING, AND I'M SORRY I DIDN'T BELIEVE IN YOU. I WOULD LIKE A MAKEUP SET. ♡ MY MOTHER SAYS I'M STILL TOO YOUNG, BUT I WANT TO BECOME MORE BEAUTIFUL AND MAKE MY BIG BROTHER FALL IN LOVE WITH ME.

YAWN...

THE HARD PART IS AFTER GETTING THEM TO SLEEP.

9 P.M.

IF YOU DON'T GO TO BED, SANTA CAN'T COME.

COME ON.

I WANT TO SLEEP NEXT TO HIM!

HUH? ONLY IF BIG BROTHER IS WITH ME!

HM?

PULL

LI' PULL

PULL

DASH

SPLISH

SPLASH

COME BACK SOON!

WE STILL HAVE TIME.

I'M GOING OUT.

Going shopping is Santa's job.

HM?

ZZZ

ZZZ

SANTA-SAN, I....

MMN...

PRESENT...

OH.

JUST SLEEP TALK.

WHEW!

YES, YES. WHAT IS IT?

U... N...

BIG BROTH-ER...?

GASP!

SHE'S WAKING UP!

SO THE ADULTS CAN HAVE PRESENTS, TOO...?

HUH?

CAN WE SPLIT MY PRES-ENT...

BIG BROTHER AND FISH-SAN ARE ALSO BEING GOOD...

THEY'LL BE LONELY IF WE LEAVE THEM OUT.

THINGS THAT DON'T HAVE SHAPE...

FOR ADULTS...

BECOME OUR PRESENTS.

SNORE...

I GET TO KEEP THOSE FEELINGS OF YOURS.

FU FU!

I'M HOME.

Next Morning.

THEY BOTH LOOK SO HAPPY!!

I'LL BE ABLE TO MAKE BIG BROTHER FALL FOR ME NOW!

MEAT

I'M GOING TO EAT IT ALL BY MYSELF!!

YEAH, THEY'RE PERFECT!!

I THINK THEY'LL LOVE THEM!!

DO YOU THINK THESE WILL WORK?

WEL-COME BACK, TATSUMI!

WHY ARE YOU SO HAPPY ALL OF A SUDDEN?

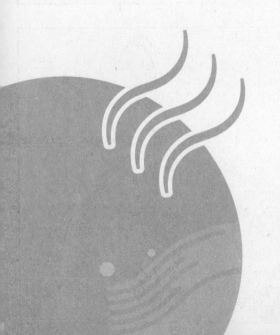

オレん家のフロ事情

RIGHT NOW, HE'S...

I KNOW, BECAUSE I'VE BEEN FRIENDS WITH HIM A LONG TIME.

HEY. WAKE UP, YOU TWO.

DEFINITELY WORRYING ABOUT SOMETHING!!

TATSU-MI HAS BEEN ACTING WEIRD.

CHAPTER **79**

SOUSUKE WORRIES ABOUT TATSUMI

BUT WHAT'S EATING AT HIM?

THAT FACE...

HE LOOKS LIKE SOMEONE WHO BROKE HIS SHOELACES AND IS WONDERING IF HE COULD STILL USE THEM.

IT'S THE EXPRESSION SOMEONE MAKES WHEN THEY SCRATCH THEIR BLUE PHONE AND THINK OF COLORING IT IN WITH BLACK MAGIC MARKER...!

OH.

NO, IT'S CHANGED!

NO, IT'S THE FACE OF SOMEONE WHO CAN'T GET HIS LUNCHBOX OPEN...!!

BECAUSE HE HAS SHORT NAILS!

MMMGH!

むきき

WHY?

ARE YOU A RETIRED OLD MAN?

THEN LET'S GO TO THE PUBLIC BATH ON THE WAY HOME!!

TAT-SUMI!!

BIING BO-ONG BEENG

I SHOULD NONCHA-LANTLY ASK HIM HOW HE'S DOING!

NO. I GET ALL I NEED AND THEN SOME.

PA-SHUNK

SEE YOU.

DON'T YOU LIKE TAKING BATHS?

YOU'RE ASKING ME WHY?

LET'S PLAY TWO-PLAYER! I HAVE A NEW GAME~!

WHAT?

TELL ME, IN TWENTY WORDS OR LESS, THE REASON A HIGH SCHOOL BOY WOULD TURN DOWN HIS BEST FRIEND'S INVITATION AND LEAVE RIGHT AFTER CLASS.

WHAT IS IT, YOU MORE UNPOPULAR HIGH SCHOOL BOY?

I HAVE A QUES-TION FOR YOU UNPOP-ULAR KIDS.

SLICE

I'M FINE.

NO.

I HATE YOU GUYS!!

DASH

WHAT MAKES YOU THINK YOU'RE HIS BEST FRIEND?

ISN'T THAT QUESTION WORDED WRONG TO BEGIN WITH?

BLIP BLIP

SOUSUKE IS WHINING AGAIN.

I NEVER GET TIRED OF WATCHING HIM.

I DON'T WANT TO BE LEFT OUT!

LET'S PLAY.

WH-WH-WH-WHEN DID HE BECOME SUCH A DELIN-QUENT...?!

WHY DID HE BUY SUCH A BIG...

I'LL INVESTIGATE HIM ON MY OWN!!

FINE!

SNEAK

SNEAK

WHAT BUSINESS DOES A SCHOOL UNIFORM HAVE HERE?

HM?

HE SAID HE DIDN'T HAVE WORK TODAY.

HM?

HM?

YOU'RE TATSUMI'S FRIEND?

UM AH

N... NO, UM...!

I SAW TATSUMI-KUN JUST A SECOND AGO...

DING

RUSTLE

I'M SCARED OF MY BIG SISTER FINDING OUT!!

NO, I'M FINE!!

WANT TO DRINK?

KIDS NOWA-DAYS ARE SO STRICT.

SHWUP

A HUGE BOTTLE OF BOOZE?!

NOTHING'S REALLY CHANGED LATELY.

BIG BROTH-ER?

HUH?

WHY?

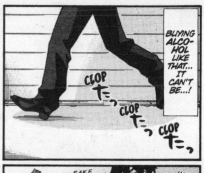

BUYING ALCOHOL LIKE THAT... IT CAN'T BE...!

CLOP

CLOP

CLOP

CLOP

HUH? BUT THIS IS SUSPICIOUS!

BLAH WORRY BLAH BLAH BLAH ALCOHOL...

BLAH BLAB BLAH...

SAKE RIGHT AFTER CLASS IS SO FREAKIN' GOOD!

HEH HEH HEH.

EVENING DRINKING EVEN THOUGH HE'S A HIGH SCHOOL KID?!

NO.

EVEN ONCE BIG BROTHER REACHES DRINKING AGE, HE WOULDN'T GO DOWN THE PATH OF ALCOHOL.

HE KNOWS NOTHING COMES OF IT!

I CAN'T BELIEVE YOU'D WALK DOWN THAT PATH.

WHAT MADE YOU BECOME THIS W--

HE SMELLS THE SAME AS USUAL. I DON'T THINK THAT ALCOHOL IS FOR DRINKING. HE MUST HAVE ANOTHER NEED FOR IT TODAY.

KASUMI-CHAN?!

SNIFF

THERE'S NO WAY I'D SURVIVE SEEING MY BIG BROTHER ONLY ONCE A MONTH.

TODAY IS A WEEKDAY...!

WHY ARE YOU HERE?!

KASUMI-CHAN!!

IT'S A SECRET!

SHH...

WHIP

I'M USELESS TO HIM IF IT'S ABOUT A GIRLFRIEND!!

No girlfriend. →

I'LL JUST HAVE TO ASK THE NEIGHBORS!

HUH?

IT ALWAYS SEEMS LIVELY OVER THERE.

WE SHOULD HAVE EATEN HIM UP WHEN HE WAS SINGLE.

SLURP

BUT IF I ASK MY SISTERS ABOUT IT...

EH, IT'S STILL NOT-TOO LATE.

OOH, SOMEONE CLAIMED HIM?

THEY'D POUNCE ON HIM.

I SEE...

OH.

BUT SOMETIMES WE CAN HEAR ANGRY YELLING.

NO, NO. I'M NOT USELESS JUST BECAUSE I DON'T HAVE A GIRLFRIEND!!

I HAVE SOME KNOWLEDGE OF GIRLS!!

THE LIGHTS ARE ON LATE EVERY NIGHT. ♡

JUST BETWEEN US.

OF COURSE, THE VOICES, TOO. ♡

TURN

RIGHT! I HAVE AN IDEA ABOUT HIS PROBLEM NOW!

ALL THAT I DON'T KNOW...

IS HOW TO MAKE HIM TALK---!

TATSU-MI...! YOU...!

HE TAKES SUCH LONG BATHS EVEN THOUGH HE'S SO YOUNG. ♡♡

GOODNESS!

CHATTER CHATTER

DON'T MAKE SUCH A BORING FACE!!

I'LL LISTEN, SO TELL ME WHAT'S BOTHERING YOU!!

YOU'LL FEEL A LITTLE BETTER!!

I DO HAVE A QUESTION TO ASK YOU.

YEAH! HM? ASK ME?

WHY AM I GETTING SO WORKED UP ANYWAY?!

IT BOTHERS ME WHEN YOU WORRY ON YOUR OWN.

SOU-SUKE...

HMPH!

HE WAS THINKING ABOUT HIS DINNER?!

WHAT THE HELL?!

BLUUUUUSH

STEWED PORK BLOCKS OR SIMMERED TRIPE. WHICH DO YOU THINK IS BETTER?

I FINALLY BOUGHT SOME GOOD COOKING WINE, BUT I CAN'T FIGURE OUT WHICH ONE I SHOULD DO.

Merman in My Tub

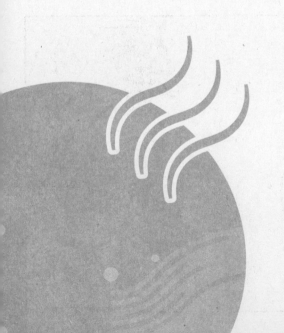

オレん家のフロ事情

MEOW

KURA-
YAMA-
SAN.

TAP
TAP

OH...

TATSUMI-
KUN!

WE'RE
TAKING
CARE OF
HER
WHILE
HER
OWNER IS
AWAY.

SHU-TAH

GYAAAH!

TONK

SPLISH SPLISH SPLISH

MEEKO-ISAAAN?!

NO

I'LL
DO
IT.

PAUSE

WELL...
THAT
IS...

UM,
I HAVE
A BIT
OF A
REQUEST...

CHAPTER 80

TO
MEEKO-SAN,
WITH LOVE

YO!!

I... I NEVER THOUGHT THE DAY I'D SEE YOU AGAIN...

WOULD EVER COME...!

DROOO

I CAME OVER TO HANG OUT-NYA~!!

RATTLE

HUH ...?!

BUT THEY REMEMBER PRETTY WELL.

I THOUGHT CATS FORGOT ABOUT PEOPLE RIGHT AWAY.

Probably how he smells.

BA-THUMP

SNIFF SNIFF SNIFF SNIFF

?!!

YOU GUYS EVEN BROUGHT A REAL CAT. YOU GUYS ARE EXCITED ABOUT THIS!!

RUB RUB

MEEKO-SAN IS REALLY HATING THIS.

I'VE NEVER SEEN HER LIKE THAT.

WHAT SHOULD I ASK ABOUT FIRST?

TA...

THE EARS ON TOP OF A RANDA-NA, HIS AGE?

KER-PLUNK

TAKASU...?!

LOUD AND TEMPER-AMENTAL?

NYA!!

LOOK, I'M THE SAME AS YOU!

SERI-OUSLY?!

IT'S ALL RIGHT, I'M NOT SCARY!!

WELL THEN, DO YOU LIKE THIS?!

THAT?

HM?

WHAT DO YOU MEAN BY ENDING WORDS IN "NYA"?!

ACTING LIKE AN ANIME CAT!

SHAKE

SHAKE

PURR MEOW~!

SO I'M CELEBRA-TING.

FEBRUARY 22ND IS CAT DAY, RIGHT?

SO HIGH! SO HIGH!

Amazed by the skills of a playboy.

SPLISH SPLISH

I FEEL A "WHY DIDN'T YOU TELL ME" STARE.

......

NYA!

STARE

I MEAN CELE-BRA-TING-NYA!

AH.

CATS DON'T HUNT THEIR OWN.

IF YOU PUT ON A CAT ACT, SHE MIGHT STOP HUNTING YOU.

MEEOW?

HUH?!

WHY SHOULD I ACT LIKE MY NATURAL ENEMY?!

HERE.

ONE FOR YOU, TOO.

THIS IS WHAT IT MEANS TO BE A CHIMERA...?!

WIGGLE-NYAN!

SPLISH-NYAN!

I SEE, NYAN! ♡

AND SO.

WE COLLECTED TALENTED KITTY EARS-NYA!

SO, WHAT SHOULD WE DO NYAOW?

WHO KNOWS?

I'VE BECOME A CAT.

GORO-MARU FORGOT TO END HIS SENTENCE-NYA. ...MINUS ONE POINT.

I...

I WILL BE THE BEST CAT HERE!!

SHO-TAP!

HEY, STOP THAT.

MAYBE WE NEED TO JUST NYAN-NYAN THE WHOLE DAY-NYA?

RAISE

MMGH!

TATSUMI IS THE LAST-NYA.

HE HATES TO LOSE.

WHY DON'T WE HAVE A KING OF MALE CATS COMPETITION THAT MEETS HER STANDARDS?!

OH!! THAT SOUNDS FUN!!

SINCE MEEKO-SAN IS HERE...

OH.

SERIOUSLY! WE'RE DEPENDING ON YOU-NYA!!

HE'S SO SERIOUS ABOUT IT!

RUMBLE RUMBLE RUMBLE RUMBLE

I HAVE TO DECIDE WHICH TOMCAT IS DESERVING OF MEEKO-SAN.

THE JUDGE

BUT WAIT... A CONTEST BETWEEN JUST THE TWO OF US?!

AND THUS, THE BATTLE BEGINS.

ROUND 2:

"THE PRIDE OF A MALE CAT."

ROUND 1:

"LIKE A CAT."

EVEN AFTER GETTING INTO WATER (WHICH YOU HATE) MERITS POINTS.

AS A CAT, HOW WILD AND MANLY YOU ARE...

ビシャ SPLASH

"GENTLE-MANLY."

"LOV-ABLE."

"GAL-LANT."

THERE ARE ALL NECESSARY QUALITIES.

OH.

HOW-EVER, EVEN MORE IMPORTANT...

MEEKO-SAN IS GOING TO GET WET...

NYAOW

A SINGLE MER-LION IS IN THE MIX.

OH.

IT LOOKS LIKE SHE CAN'T SEE HIM.

ARE YOU ALL RIGHT-NYA?

UM.

...IS THE ABILITY TO PROTECT.

CATS DON'T HAVE GREAT DAY VISION.

?!

?!

But her only interest in him was as food!

Male allure was something he didn't have...!

PULL

HEH.

So desirably cold!

Meeko scoffs at the sight of him!

Cold!

CRIES?

MERROW!

TATSUMI IS SO INTO IT!!

Her form is more gallant and dignified than any of these toothless males...!

FWUP

FROM OUTSIDE...?!

WHO DARES TO JUMP IN AT A TIME LIKE THIS?!

AND ROUND 3! ROUND 4:

WAHHHH

DIGNITY

CONK

The battle grows more intense.

TWITCH

COORDINATION.

CONK

I HAVE ALREADY CHOSEN MY BRIDE.

BITE

The type that likes newcomers-nya.

EVEN THOUGH SHE'S KNOWN ME LONGER!

SHE'S NOT ATTRACTED TO ME AT ALL...!

WHAT ABOUT THIS?!

THEN...

Showing his abs in a desperate pose.

OF COURSE SHE WOULD TAKE THAT BAIT!!

THAT'S NOT FAIR, WAKASA!!

MEOW!

HEEK! SHE'S SO SCARY!!

HE'S SO BRAVE, I COULD NEVER DO THAT...!

GA RUSTLE

GA RATTLE!!!

TOO BAD.

CHUCKLE

YOU HAVE TOO MUCH COMPETITION. WE'VE BEEN TRYING TO WIN HER HEART FOR HOURS...

SORRY, STRAY-KUN.

NYA-MEOW

FIDGET

FIDGET

WITHDRAW...

It seems the real thing is number one.

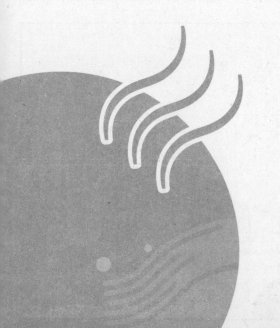

オレん家のフロ事情

CHAPTER 81

MEETING MAKARA
~PART 1~

A MER--

MER-BOY?

SQUEEZE

TICK

TICK

TICK

......

WHAT DO YOU MEAN, "FINALLY"?!

SPLISH

DO YOU SEE ME AS THAT KIND OF PERSON, TATSUMI?!

SPLISH

DIIIING!

THAT'S SURPRIS-ING EVEN TO ME.

SO, I FINALLY MEET YOUR ILLEGITIMATE CHILD.

S...

SORRY, TATSUMI.

HE'S REALLY SUSPICIOUS OF ME.

HIS NAME IS MAKARA.

I TOOK CARE OF HIM FOR A WHILE WHEN HE WAS SMALL.

HE'S LIKE A LITTLE BROTHER OR JUNIOR TO ME!!

MAKARA...

GOOD BOY...

HE'S A LITTLE SHY AND REALLY TERRITORIAL, BUT HE'S A GOOD KID...

POFF

POFF

DID I SAY SOMETHING STRANGE?

HM?

INSTEAD OF HIM TAKING CARE OF YOU?

CARE OF HIM...?

TOOK...

HMM...

THE ORANGE THE COLORS WHITE AND BLACK PATTERNS...

AND HE'S TERRITORIAL AND LOVES TO HIDE...

GRAR!

RAISE

ARE YOU GOING TO EAT, TOO?

WELL, WE'LL LEAVE IT AT THAT.

TATSUMI!!

They become aggressive when they are in their home territory.

RUB RUB RUB

TOUSLE

A CLOWNFISH, HUH.

YOUR HAIR LOOKS LIKE A SEA ANEMONE TO HIM.

SPLISH SPLISH

HE REMINDS ME OF A CERTAIN SENPAI...

GRAR

GRAR

GRAR

FOOD...

HUMAN...

TRAP...

GRAR

HE'S NOT A POKÉ-MON.

YOU ALMOST CAUGHT HIM!

AAH! SO CLOSE!!

COME HERE ... I CAN!

SQUEEZE

IT'S A LOT OF TROU-BLE~!

MY HAIR ALWAYS GETS SO TOUSLED WHEN MAKARA IS AROUND.

TOUSLE

YOU DON'T LOOK DIFFERENT FROM NORMAL.

I WON'T ...

They form a symbiotic relationship with anemones and dislike leaving.

Clown fish.

LET GO, ANY-MORE...

I SEE.

HE HASN'T CHANGED AT ALL.

HE GETS REALLY LONELY AND HE LIKES TO BE SPOILED, SO I WAS WORRIED...

BUT I CAN'T ALWAYS BE WITH YOU...

I'M HAPPY YOU LIKE ME.

YOU'RE RIGHT!!

OH!

ISN'T THAT PRETTY AMAZ-ING?

BUT HE CAME HERE BY HIM-SELF.

MAKA-RA...

AMAZ-ING...?

TWITCH

SOMEHOW HIS WORDS DON'T SEEM CONVINC-ING.

I'M SO WORRIED ABOUT YOU.

YOU'VE ALREADY GROWN UP, SO YOU HAVE TO BE ABLE TO LIVE ON YOUR OWN...!!

OH? HE'S OPENING UP...?

GLANCE GLANCE

AH.

SLIP

WAKA——!

OUT WE GO.

THEN...

SHOULDN'T WE JUST TAKE THAT TERRITORY AWAY FROM HIM?

!

WAKA-SA...!

WATCH OUT.

GRAB

ARE YOU ALL RIGHT?

AH...

AH...!

......

I'M OKAY. WAKA-SA.

AND...

FLOP

FLOP

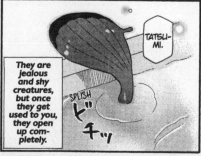

TATSU-MI.

They are jealous and shy creatures, but once they get used to you, they open up completely.

SPLISH

SO HE'S CLUMSY, HUH?

WAKA-SA!

HE'S NOT HAVING A TANTRUM.

HE'S TRYING TO SWIM.

WAKA-SA!

FLOP

FLOP

Watching over him.

SPLISH

MAKARA ADULT!!

SPLISH

BEAM

HIGH-FIVE!

YOU'VE GROWN UP A LITTLE MORE, MAKARA!!

GREAT!!

......

SIZZLE

WHEN YOU'RE WITH A LITTLE KID LIKE THAT, YOU ACT MORE LIKE AN ADULT.

Cooking more food.

WAIT!!

DON'T OPEN THE DOOR, TATSU-MI!!

THE ★ VEGETA-BLES!

SORRY FOR MAKING YOU WAIT.

RUSTLE

GA-CHAK

HOW MANY TIMES ARE YOU GOING TO TRY THAT? GOODNESS.

KYAA!!

?!!

Merman
in My Tub

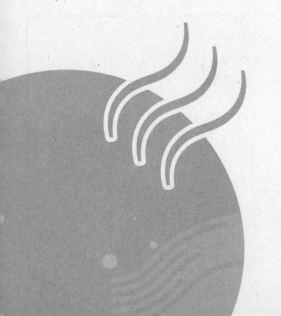

オレん家のフロ事情

...TA-TSUMI.

MADE MAKARA INTO A WOMAN...

SQUEEZE

B...

B-B-B-BIG BROTH-ER...

TH-TH-THAT WOM-AN...

HUH?!

Y-YOU GOT IT WRONG!

SHWOOM

BIG BROTHER MADE YOU INTO A WOMAN?!!

WHAT DO YOU MEAN—?!

HE... WAS A MAN UNTIL JUST NOW...

SHAKE SHAKE SHAKE

HUH...?

WOMAN...?

CHAPTER 82
MEETING MAKARA
~PART 2~

Clown fish.

Depending on their environment, they are fish that can change genders.

HOW IN THE WORLD CAN I BE CALM?!

FLUSTER

FLUSTER

CALM DOWN, LITTLE SISTER!

THIS CHILD'S NAME IS MAKARA AND--!

W- WAIT, LITTLE SISTER...!

FINALLY.

FWAP

ANY WAY YOU LOOK AT IT...

THIS LOOKS BAD!!

MY!

THIS DAY HAS FINALLY COME...

THA-THUMP

THA-THUMP

SEDU-CING MY BROTHER!

FIDGET

FIDGET

FLINCH

AN EVIL WOMAN ....!!

BOUNCE

SEE --?!!

MA...

MAKA-RA...?

I'VE NEVER SEEN YOU ACT LIKE THAT BEFORE...

I WON'T LOSE!!

FLAP

THE FIGHT HAS JUST BEGUN!!

WAAAAH

I WON'T...

I...

E- EVIL... WOMAN ....!

FLAP

WHAT?

ARE YOU TRYING TO GET IN MY WAY?

I WANT TO... THANK HIM.

PULL

YOU'RE GOING TO WATCH A MOVIE WITH ME NOW, BIG BROTHER!!

NO!!

LET'S GO, BIG BROTH-ER!!

SAVED...

MAKA-RA...

GAVE...

CLOTHES.

WAIT...

TUG

NO ONE...

ELSE...

TATSU-MI. SO WONDER-FUL...

MA-KARA'S HOUSE

VERY PRETTY...

COME VISIT...?

THIS PERSON UNDER-STANDS.

I CAN ONLY HOLD MY BREATH FOR ABOUT A MINUTE.

HE WON'T COME!!

STOP TRYING TO DRAG MY BROTHER INTO THE SEA!!

By the way, Makara's "house" is twenty meters below sea level.

THAT'S THE PROB-LEM?

YEAH.

WANT TO EAT BREAK-FAST?

GROWL

GOODNESS!

YEAH...

THAT WAS SCARY...!

NO.

JUST...

WHAT'S SO FUNNY?

FU FU.

I CAN'T BELIEVE YOU'D TRY TO SEDUCE BIG BROTHER WITH THESE THINGS!!

OH!

WHAT...!

IN THE SEA, HE ALWAYS HID BEHIND ME AND NEVER MOVED ON HIS OWN.

BUT *NOW*, HE'S FIGHTING WITH YOUR LITTLE SISTER.

CLATTER

LET GO!

OR ELSE...

HEY, DON'T FIGHT...

DON'T BE SO COCKY JUST BECAUSE I DON'T HAVE THEM!!

THAT'S TRUE.

CLATTER CLATTER

MAKARA WINS...

THEN...

HEEK!

IF YOU DO IT THAT STRONGLY...!

ST...

STOP IT~!

IT'S LONELY BEING A BIG BROTHER.

EVERYONE GROWS UP AND GOES AWAY LIKE THIS.

OUCH!

HUFF!

HUFF!

SPLISH

SPLISH

DON'T SHOW OFF THOSE BIG *THINGS* OF YOURS!!

MNGH!

YOU'RE RIGHT ABOUT THAT.

WELL...

I KNOW, RIGHT?

SLUMP

DON'T TAKE MY BIG BROTHER!!

AY...

BIG BROTHER IS REALLY SOFT-HEARTED ABOUT FISH RIGHT NOW!!

?!

TATSU-MI.

WAKA-SA.

ALWAYS TOGETH-ER...

D-DID YOU GET MAD?

HUH?

WHAM

THAT *SCREAM* JUST NOW!

WHAT HAP-PENED?!

PLAY.

SHAKE

SHAKE

ONLY TRIPPED...

MA...

MAKARA DIDN'T ATTACK...

GOOD BOY...

GASP!!

BUT TURNS INTO A **MAN** NEAR A HUMAN WOMAN.

TURNS INTO A WOMAN AROUND A HUMAN MALE.

MAKARA...

WHAT'S GOING ON?

OH?

I'M **NOT** LYING...!!

HE'S LYING!!

UWAAAAH!

WAAAAAH!

TEE HEE!

YOU SHOULD HAVE *SAID SO* FROM THE BEGIN-NING!!

GOODNESS!!

GLARE

オレん家のフロ事情

THUMP

THERE YOU GO.

WOW, AMAZING!!

HOT SPRING BASE

LIKE A HOT SPRING

YOU'RE LAZY, BUT STILL *PRETTY* HEALTHY, AREN'T YOU?

DON'T YOU WANT TO BECOME HEALTHY...?

TATSUMI...

WHAT IS IT?

YOU'RE PRETTY AGGRESSIVE TODAY.

?

SPLISH

THAT'S NOT WHAT I MEAN!!

OR A GOOD MASSAGE? THAT'S WHAT I'M SAYING!!

DON'T YOU NEED A BATH?

......

THAT'S NOT WHAT I MEAN!!

CHAPTER 83

MERMAN IN MY TUB STYLE HEALTH SPA

I WAS THINKING IT'D BE NICE IF YOU GOT HEALTHY, TOO!

NO, I'M ACTUALLY HEALTHY ALREADY.

IT SEEMS THERE ARE PLACES CALLED HEALTH SPAS.

I SEE.

HEALTHY FOR ME?

HM?

RIGHT!

PERFECT HEALTH~!

WHERE DID THESE CLOTHES COME FROM?!

I'LL MAKE YOU RELAX TODAY!!

LEAVE IT TO ME!

THUMBS UP!

YOU ALWAYS TAKE CARE OF ME, TATSUMI!

HM?

ROPE?

ATTACHED TO THE BAND?

ENJOY. ♥

HI SPLASH

I'M GOING TO GET PREPARED.

RIGHT.

PREPARED?

IT'S LEADING INTO THE BATHROOM.

GA-CHAK

IS HE ALL RIGHT?

IS THERE SOME MEANING IN HIS CROSS DRESSING?

HEALTH SPA

JUST ONE TODAY?

WELCOME. ♥

RECEPTION

WIGGLE

WIGGLE

MY.

THOSE CLOTHES FIT YOU PERFECTLY. ♥

THANK GOODNESS. ♥

HERE! ♥

PLEASE PUT ON THIS BAND. ♥

CLOSE

NOW, COME RIGHT THIS WAY~! ♥ ♥

OH...

He's realized.

Y...

YEAH...

A UNIFORM, EVEN. WHAT IS THIS SERIOUS ATTITUDE OF HIS...?

I HAVE A BAD FEELING.

SHWAA!

IT'S EMBAR-RASSING.

SO PLEASE DON'T STARE *TOO* MUCH...!

OH. IT'S GOOD.

HOW IS THE STRENGTH...?

I SEE. THAT'S GOOD...

THEN I WILL DO YOUR WHOLE BODY NOW!

HUH?

SPLASH

POKE POKE POKE POKE POKE POKE POKE POKE POKE

Under the umbrella are many tentacles that numb the body.

UHEEEEEEEK...

MY... MY EYES ARE...!

YEAH, THAT'S IMPORTANT.

NEXT, SOME SCALP MASSAGE.

RATTLE

ROLL

DAZE

HM? EVEN YOU, AGARI-SAN?

SNAAP

DO WHAT-EVER YOU WANT.

NEXT IS A LEG MASS-AGE!

LIFT

STRAIGHTEN

PLEASE STEP ON IT FREELY TO RE-LEASE SOME STRESS.

IF YOU DON'T MIND USING MY CRAPPY SHELL...

IT IS OUR FAMOUS EXFOLIATING MASSAGE. ♡

SCRUB
SCRUB
SCRUB
SCRUB
SCRUB

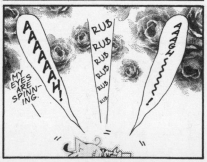

AAAAAH!

RUB
RUB
RUB
RUB
RUB

AAAGH~!

MY EYES ARE SPINN-ING.

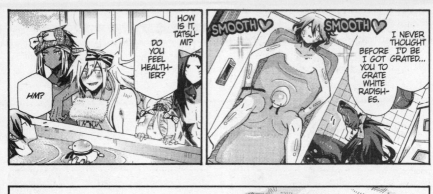

YAWN!

MM.

DON'T WANNA.

LEMME STAY LIKE THIS.

SLUMP

I AM EXHAUSTED...

WE WORKED REALLY HARD.

YEAH.

A few hours later.

TATSUMI-SAN.

PLEASE WAKE UP SOON?

WHEW~!

SHAKE

SHAKE

DINNER.

READY YET?

I'M HUNGRY.

It seems dinner was very late this day.

WE TURNED TATSUMI REALLY LAZY!!

TA...

TOSS

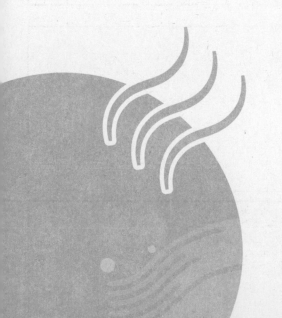

オレん家のフロ事情

YOU SAY...?!

NO, NO. SOME-ONE LIKE ME... SLOW AND CLUMSY...

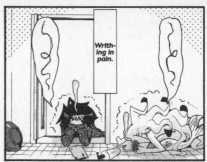

Writhing in pain.

ARE YOU LISTEN-ING?!

FWUP

I'M FAST ENOUGH TO KEEP UP WITH SENPAI! SHARKS, TOO!

THIS FORM OF MINE IS AS GRACEFUL AS A PORPOISE.

IS THAT SO?

SLIP

S... SORRY.

YOU SLIPPED AGAIN?

BECAUSE OF YOUR FISH SLIME.

TH-THE TILES ARE SLIPPERY!

SPLISH
SPLISH
SPLISH

JEEZ... YOU'RE WAY TOO SLOW AND CLUMSY.

YEAH, YEAH. I HAVE TO CLEAN THE ROOMS.

TA-

TATSUMI, YOU IDIOT!!

BA-THUNK

WHY DO YOU LOOK SO SUR-PRISED...?

SLOW AND CLUMSY?!

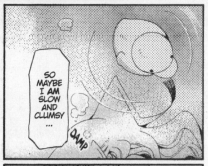

SO MAYBE I AM SLOW AND CLUMSY ...

DAMP

NUDGE NUDGE

DAMP

DAMP

DAMP

A MERMAN WHO SLIPS AND TRIPS SHOULD JUST STILL STAY INSIDE THE TUB. *HEH HEH HEH...*

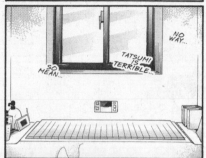

NO WAY...

TATSUMI IS TERRIBLE...

SO MEAN...

DAMP

DAMP

DAMP

I SHOULD JUST LIVE ALL ALONE IN THE DARK...

AHH!

IT'S DARK...

BLUB

BLUB

BLUB

HUH...?

SOME-HOW... IT'S CALM-ING.

WH...

WHO...?

!

IT'S FINE.

TO BE THAT WAY.

MA... MAKI ...?!

WHEN DID YOU ...?!

I DIDN'T NOTICE.

WHERE WAS HE?

I'M SORRY! I ACTUALLY CAME OVER TO PLAY TWO DAYS AGO. I HAVE SO MUCH NERVE THAT IT'S RIDICULOUS, I KNOW...!!!

THERE'S NO NEED TO FORCE YOURSELF OUT INTO THE LIGHT.

I MIGHT SLIP AGAIN IF I GO OUT.

IT'S BEST TO STAY IN HERE, HUH?

NOD NOD

I SEE...

YES, THAT'S HOW IT IS.

IS THAT HOW IT IS?

TATSUMI STILL GETS GOOSEBUMPS WHEN I TOUCH HIM.

SHELLS ARE NICE THAT WAY.

YOU CAN HIDE AWAY AS MUCH AS YOU WANT.

AND HE PUTS BELL PEPPERS INSIDE THE HAMBURGER STEAK...

OOOH!

YOU'RE GOING TO BECOME ONE?

I MUST BE MEANT TO BE A SHELLFISH!!

EH HEH HEH

AH HA HA

THE HUMAN WORLD IS HARSH...

MAYBE HE HATES ME...

DAMP DAMP

I WON'T GO OUT!!

× ×

YEAH! I SHOULD JUST STAY LIKE THIS FOR- EVER!!

BEING A SHELL- FISH IS NICE...

RE- UNION ?!

THANK YOU, WAKASA.

I WAS ALSO DEPRESS- ED...

BECAUSE I WASN'T INVITED TO THE REUNION.

NO ONE BOTHERS YOU.

NO ONE MAKES FUN OF YOU.

NO ONE COMES TO VISIT!!

"WHY DIDN'T YOU COME LAST TIME?"

"OH, MAKI!"

THE DESPAIR I FELT FINDING OUT AFTER THE FACT.

"HUH...?"

IF I LEAVE, I LOSE THE GAME...

POKE

あぁぁ

OH NOOO...!

MAKES YOU JUST WANT TO DIE...

REAL- LY...

HEH HEH...

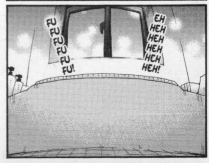

FU FU FU FU FU FU!

EH HEH HEH HEH HEH HEH!

DURING THE FIGHT BETWEEN TAKASU AND ECHIZEN...

MY EFFORTS TO STOP THEM WERE ALL IN VAIN.

HUH? YOU WERE THERE?!

※Chapter 76.

OH!

MERRY CHRISTMAS!

THERE WERE ALSO TIMES THE WINDOW WAS CLOSED AND I COULDN'T GET IN...

TAP

TAP

※Chapter 78.

I HAD TO LOOK AWAY WHEN MAKARA CHANGED, AND HID IN MY SHELL...

HUH? THAT TIME, TOO?!

※Chapter 81.

EVER NOTICED ME AT ALL...

BUT NO ONE...

MAYBE I'M JUST BEING TOO COCKY...

SOMEONE LIKE ME, TRYING TO JOIN IN WITH EVERYONE ELSE.

MUMBLE

MUMBLE

Hand that doesn't know where to go.

GA-CHAK

HEY.

AHHHH...

BUT, UM, AHH...

HUH?

HUH?

THE LID IS CLOSED.

IT'S TIME TO EAT.

Wakasa decided the shellfish lifestyle wasn't for him.

LET'S EAT!!

SPLASH

オレん家のフロ事情

I DON'T REALLY HATE ANY FOODS.

YOU EVEN PINCHED MY NOSE!! SO MEAN!!

WHEEZE

MMN-NPH!! MMMPH!! <HOW'D YOU LIKE IT IF I FED YOU FOODS YOU HATED?!>

MN ....!

WHEEZE

FWING

Meat-stuffed bell peppers.

YOU'RE TOO MUCH OF A CHILD.

THEY'RE ONLY GREEN AND YELLOW VEGETA-BLES.

PULL

PULL

CRACK CRACK

COME ON OVER AND I'LL PET YOU.

I SEE... SO YOU'RE AN ADULT?

OKAY. DINNER IS FIN-ISHED.

ZUWOSH

SPLISH WAKASA'S

STOP

BLEAH!

CHAPTER 85

MAKARA'S LOVE

MAKA-RA. YOU'RE A BIG GIRL RIGHT NOW.

YOU SHOULDN'T HUG A BOY SO EASILY.

EDGE...

WE'RE TOTALLY DIFFERENT SIZES, RIGHT?

SORRY, TATSU-MI... I CHECKED THE DIF-FERENCE WITH WAKA-SA...

AH HA HA!

THEY MIGHT MISUNDER-STAND YOU.

WRONG.

MISUN-DER-STAND.

HUH?

SHOULD WE CHANGE THE TITLE OF THIS CHAPTER?!

EEEK!

DOES IT NEED A MATURE RATING!

PUSH

NO GOOD?

NO.

MAKARA IS A FISH.

......

YOU MIGHT BE A PROPER ADULT...

......

YOU DID NOTHING WRONG.

I THINK YOU'RE CUTE.

BUT...

I STILL DON'T KNOW WHAT LOVE IS.

BUT I KNOW IT'S NOT A QUESTION YOU ANSWER EASILY.

I'M STILL A KID.

TATSU-MI.

A KID...?

YEAH.

See you in Volume 7!

REPORT ON DUBBING OF MERMAN IN MY TUB ANIME ~PART 2~

I BELIEVE YOU ALL SHOULD BE WATCHING THE ANIME ALREADY, BUT HERE IS THE SECOND HALF OF MY REPORT!!

YOU ARE WATCHING, RIGHT?!

TAKASU'S COCKY ATTITUDE WAS WONDERFUL! HE ALWAYS LIVENED UP THE SCENE!!

I LAUGHED AT ALMOST EVERY SCENE HE APPEARED IN.

I LOVE THE "HEY!" IN EPISODE 3 NO MATTER HOW MANY TIMES I WATCH IT.

REPEAT REPEAT

HEY!

YO, HAPPY NEW YEAR.

Takasu Role
Tatsuhisa Suzuki

EDITOR

GRAB

NEXT IS MA--

AH!!

GLUG GLUG

DRINKING THE ENTIRE TIME

J-JUST A LITTLE!

I SECRETLY WISHED THAT TAKASU WOULD SING ALONG WITH WAKASA.

DURING THE TUB PARTY IN EPISODE 11...

BIG BROTHER...

AND THE ONLY GIRL AMONG ALL THE GUYS WAS THE SUPER ADORABLE KASUMI ...!!!

LET'S TAKE A BATH TOGETHER!

SHAKING

SHE EXUDED SO MUCH SISTERLY LOVE! IT WAS ADORABLE AGAIN GREAT!!

Kasumi Role
Ibuki Kido

WHEN I HEARD HIS SUPER LOW MUMBLE...

IT WAS AMAZING.

I COULDN'T HELP JUST LISTENING LIKE A FAN!!

THANK YOU, VERY MUCH!!

THERE'S A HUMAN.

THE WORST...

WHAT A WONDERFUL VOICE... BUT IT WAS SO MUMBLY!

NO...

I WASN'T SURE HOW THE VOICE ACTOR WOULD MATCH WITH MAKI AND I WAS VERY EXCITED TO SEE.

TEE HEE!

Maki Role
Kenjiro Tsuda

THOSE WORDS EXPRESS MY HONEST OPINION ON HIS MAKI-MAKINESS!!

WHAT A WASTE NOT TO HEAR HIM LIKE THAT!!!

OH, SERIOUSLY AMAZING.

AND THEN HE SUDDENLY CHANGED TO SUCH A PLEASANT PERSONALITY.

PAH HA HA!

SO BIG!

LOOM

NARA KENKO LAND

APRIL 5TH HAS ARRIVED!!

SO MANY PEOPLE!

CHATTER CHATTER

INSIDE.

April 5: Umehara-san Talk Show
April 12: Itokichi Autograph Event
(With Mini-Talk Show)

A DAY IN MARCH.

STRAIGHTEN

I REALLY WANT TO GO AND PLAY!

I HAVE TO WATCH AND STUDY UMEHARA-SAN'S TALK SHOW TO PREPARE FOR THE 12TH!!

THE FIRST MERMAN IN MY TUB EVENT!!

I WAS SO EXCITED, I COULDN'T SLEEP!!

WENT TO NARA HEALTH SPA REPORT

• B G M •
Matenrou Opera-san Live DVD

VROOM!

~ I SELFISHLY WENT IN MY OWN CAR! ~

YAY!

MERMAN IN MY TUB SET.

FRIEND

FRIEND

HEALTH SPA INFORMATION

うぃい!
CHEEEEK!!

MANUSCRIPT HALL.

ANIME STORYBOARDS.

SO THAT'S HOW THEY'RE MADE!!

FROM THE ENTRANCE

WHOA!

TV

MERMAN IN MY TUB FANS COMMINGLED WITH THE HEALTH SPA PEOPLE!!

IT WAS FILLED WITH MERMAN IN MY TUB FROM THE FIRST FLOOR.

MERMAN IN MY TUB POSTER !?

OOOH!!

EVEN UP THE STAIRS

MUSIC MUSIC

LIKE THAT.

KIND PEOPLE HELPED ME. THANK YOU!!!

OH.

MIKUNI IS AT THE GAME CENTER.

STAMP RALLY

YOU HAVE TO FIND THE FIVE TUB MEMBER PANELS!!

YOU CAN RECEIVE OIL BLOTTING PAPERS AS A REWARD.

AND THE STAMP RALLY I ALWAYS WANTED !!

SNAP

I FOUND MAKI!!

SUPER HIDDEN

I WAS ABLE TO GET THEM BOTH!!

WE'RE STILL LOOKING FOR MAKI...

TAKASU PANEL

AND SO MANY GOODS FOR SALE!!

THE POT LUCK WAS PERFECT, TOO.

I CAN'T FIND MIKUNI OR MAKI!!

WHILE I PANICKED...

FIRST HAKUTAKA

SO FAST...

THE FIRST HAKUTAKA BULLET TRAIN COMMUTE

I WENT TO THE SHINJUKU ANIMATE ON APRIL 26TH FOR A TALK EVENT.

A GREAT DAY FOR THE TUB!

I BELIEVE SOMETHING AMAZING WILL HAPPEN!

LOOM...

WHAT THE...

ANIMATE?

HOW MANY FLOORS IS THIS...?

GUNFINISHED STORYBOARD!

GLIMMER

SOUND ROOM

I GREETED EVERYONE BEFORE THE EVENT.

AFTER A SHORT MEETING...

ITOKICHI-SAN, WHAT ABOUT THE SCRIPT?

SO BRIGHT!!

WHOA!

THE MOST NERVE-RACKING PART.

I SAT IN THE FRONT LIKE A NORMAL FAN. ☆

THEY WEREN'T IN A TUB LIKE ON THE DVD SPECIAL, BUT...

OVER 100 PEOPLE GATHERED IN A BEAUTIFUL HALL!!

AMAZING!!

GO

IT CONTINUES! ☆

MATENROU OPERA × MERMAN IN MY TUB

TALK EVENT

THANK YOU! ♥

DVD

CD

LIVE SCRIPT READING!!

THEY KEPT MAKING EVERYONE BURST INTO LAUGHTER, THEN--

AH HA HA!

THIS IS OUR SECOND MERMAN IN MY TUB EVENT, SO WE GOT THIS!!

NO SCRIPT!

TATSUMI ROLE: SHIMAZAKI-SAN

WAKASA ROLE: UMEHARA-SAN

UMEHARA-SAN STARTED THE SHOW.

AND SHIMAZAKI-SAN WORKED WITH HIM TO LIVEN UP THE CROWD.

LETTER

SLIP

AND THEN...

THE SURPRISING REVERSE VERSION, TOO!!

STAFF WORKER'S HAND

NN!

WHAT...?♥

"SINCE WE HAVE THE CHANCE, WHY NOT DO IT AGAIN WITH THE ROLES REVERSED."

IT SAYS.

CHANGE

HIS MOANS EMBARRASSED EVERYONE A BIT.

AH!

SO EROTIC!!

GRIN GRIN

GOT USED TO IT.

*DEPICTION

TATSUMI'S SLIME EXPERIENCE

ANIME SCRIPT WRITER AYANA YUNIKO-SAN WROTE THE SCRIPT FOR IT.

MY THUMBS WERE UP THE WHOLE TIME.

GJ! GJ!!

I'M GOING TO TOUCH YOU...

Y-YEAH.

OKAY...?

THEY ALSO WATCHED THE SPECIAL ANIMATION.

THE CEILING OF THE BATHROOM BROKE.

WHY DID YOU LEAVE IT ALONE?

SHIMA

*PLEASE WATCH THE DVD TO GET THE DETAILS.

OF ALL THE COMMENTS, UMEHARA-SAN'S COMMENT ON THAT ENDED UP LEAVING THE GREATEST IMPRESSION ON ME.

DUCKY-CHAN WAS SO FUNNY DURING THE DUBBING.

AND SECRET STORIES ABOUT THE MAKING OF THE ANIME WERE TOLD.

I WASN'T SURE WHETHER I SHOULD USE A HIGHER OR LOWER PITCH ON THE FIRST DAY.

GOODNESS...

THEY WATCHED THE LAST EPISODE WHILE DOING LIVE COMMENTARY. ☆

OH, IT'S TSUDA-SAN.

GIGOLO

CHATTER

*DEPICTION

NNGH

NNNGH!!

AHH

EVERYONE BURST INTO LAUGHTER AT SHIMAZAKI-SAN'S ACT AS WAKASA.

IT WAS A RARE VOICE THAT COULD ONLY BE HEARD HERE!!

HA HA!!

HA HA!!

SUCH A MANLY WAKASA!

REPORT ON DUBBING OF THE DRAMA CD

TOKYO

IT'S BEEN A WHILE SINCE I'VE BEEN TO THE CITY!

EDITOR

↑ TO GET STREET PASS FOR DRAQUE 8.

IF YOU BUY A DRAMA CD...

THE FIRST DRAMA CD!!

MERMAN IN MY TUB!

CD

I INTRUDED ON THEIR RECORDING. ☆

ANOTHER BIG EVENT CAME!!

WHILE I WAS RELAXING AFTER THE ANIME AND EVENTS...

YOU ALSO GET VOLUME 6 OF MERMAN IN MY TUB!!

THE CONTENTS:
・ECHIZEN'S APPEARANCE
・ECHIZEN'S MOLTING
・ECHIZEN VS. TAKASU
THREE STORIES FILLED WITH ECHIZEN!

REVERE ME.

BEG FOR FORGIVE-NESS.

GET ON YOUR KNEES!

HMPH!

ECHI-ZEN'S ROLE, YUSA KOUJI-SAN, JOINED.

Echizen Role
Kōji Yusa

BUT HIS SUPER SADISTIC AND EROTIC VOICE...

CHATTER

CHATTER

THE REGULAR MEMBER TAKASU...

AND TATSUMI WORKED TOGETHER WITH HIM TO CREATE A GREAT RESULT!!

ACTUALLY, UMEHARA-SAN HAD TO RECORD SEPARATELY. THE "EXTRA" IS "FUNNY" TO "LISTEN" TO!

YES !!!

PANG

MADE ME ENERGETIC AND BEGGING FOR MORE. THAT'S HOW SADISTIC-ALLY EROTIC IT WAS...!!

I FELT REALLY BAD MAKING HIM DO THE ROLE OF A MERE CRAB...

EEK

IN THE BEGIN-NING...

AND OF COURSE HIS COOL SCENES!!

FROM SUPER-SADISTIC TO COMICAL.

IT WAS VERY INTERESTING!!

BOOM!

HH HH HHHHH... HH HH HHHHH...

I'M MOLTING!!

AND THEN...

HIS HEAVY BREATH-ING...

(CHAPTER 02)

SHANK!!!

SO COOL!

FLUTTER

HE DID HIS OWN SOUND EFFECTS DURING HIS BATTLE WITH TATSUMI, TOO!!

THEY ALSO FIGHT JUST BY TURNING AWAY AND SAYING, "HMPH!"

AND THEN.

UGH-GH-GH-GH-GH!

PUNCH

PUNCH

PUNCH

COME ON! COME ON!

AFTERIMAGE

AFTERIMAGE

※ DEPICTION

ALMOST TO THE POINT YOU FORGET IT'S A TUB MANGA ...!!

THEIR FIGHT BOUNCED BACK AND FORTH PERFECT-LY.

WIGGLE

HEY!

AND THEN TAKASU AP-PEARS !!

Takasu Role: Tatsuhisa Suzuki

THE FLASHBACK TO WHEN THEY WERE CHILDREN WAS UNBEAR-ABLE...!!

YOU HAVE TO LISTEN! YOU'LL NEVER HAVE ANOTHER CHANCE ...!!

IT ALMOST MADE ME A LOVER OF LITTLE-BOY LOVE STORIES.

AND FROM THAT.

THE CHANGE TO THEIR HONEST SELVES WAS AMAZ-ING!!

HOW NOS-TALGIC!

IT WAS FUN!

AMAZ-ING...

I FELT A FRESH BREEZE...

NO, ALREADY, I'M GOING TO OVERFLOW. BATH SALTS. NUMBER THIRTEEN.

THE LAST SCENE WITH WAKASA WAS ALSO VERY CUTE. ☆

HE READ THE NAME OF THE BATH SALTS THAT CONTAINED ♡ IN THE SCRIPT STIFFLY, WHICH MADE IT SOUND VERY MISCHIEVOUS.

TAT-SUMI, WHO REINS THE TWO OF THEM IN.

HIS UN-SHAKING PRESENCE COULD EASILY BE FELT.

'HE'S LIKE THEIR DAD.'

GRAB

GRAB

Tatsumi Role:
Nobunaga Shimazaki

DESPITE EVERY-THING HE PUTS UP WITH...

HE STILL SHOWS HIS BROTHERLY SIDE AND STAYS SO COOL. PLEASE LOOK FORWARD TO IT. ☆

WAKASA GETS STUCK BETWEEN THESE THREE.

NNGH

OF COURSE HE REALLY NICE SOUNDS.

YES!

I THINK HE'S EVEN CUTER THAN HE WAS BEFORE...!!!

(PERSONAL OPINION)

Wakasa Role:
Yūichirō Umehara

PLEASE PICK UP THE SPECIAL VOLUME 6 THAT COMES ALONG WITH THE DRAMA CD!!

I SUS-PECTED IT, BUT THAT IS THE MOMENT I WAS SURE.

THIS PERSON IS A NATURAL DITZ.

I HEARD HIS RE-SPONSE...

A SIDE NOTE. ONE OF THE QUESTIONS WAS, "WHAT IS YOUR FAVORITE SEAFOOD?"

CAN I ANSWER "FRIED SHRIMP"?

HMM

SEA-FOOD, HUH?

THEY ANSWERED THREE QUESTIONS!!

A VOLUMI-NOUS, WONDER-FUL ONE!!

AND AS A SPECIAL, THE CD HAS A CAST TALK AS WELL.

PLEASE LISTEN TO FIND OUT WHAT THEY SAID. ♡

◆END◆

オレん家の ウラ事情
THE BACKGROUND OF MY HOUSE special

REQUEST 1 I WANT TO SEE THIS KIND OF ILLUSTRATION.
ITOKICHI-SENSEI'S ILLUSTRATION IS ON THE INSIDE COVER.☆

REQUEST 2 READER'S ILLUSTRATION CORNER
I'D LIKE TO SHOW YOU SOME OF THE WONDERFUL ART PEOPLE HAVE SENT ME!!

P.N neo

P.N かむかむ

P.N めがね

P.N ぶなしめじ

P.N にゃん太

たくみ大好きです。
たくみの赤面画はヤバい・・・
かわいい////
もっとたくみの
出番ふやして
ください!!

PN 黒ネジ

PN りょうた

PN りさ

オレん家のフロ事情

鷹巣もいしきちなはも
大好きです!!
ずっと応援してます!!

タコは好きか?

PN 佐藤千紘

PN 向日葵

PN 京

PN 腹巻パンダ

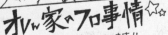

オレん家のフロ事情☆☆

アニメ化 おめでとうございます!!
何といってもキャストさんが豪華っ(*´∀`)♡
みんなとってもかわいくって癒されてます!
これからもずっと応援します(*´▽`*)

PN 黒蘭

あけましておめでとうございます!
オレフロ
6
巻 おめでとですね!!

PN 杠黄昏

REQUEST 3 QUESTIONS FOR ITOKICHI-SENSEI CORNER

Q **WHAT IS THE INSIDE OF THE BOTTOM HALF OF TAKASU, WAKASA, AND AGARI-SAN LIKE? DO THEY HAVE ONE OF *THOSE*? (MATSUOKA FUUMA)**

Their bottom halves are as edible as you'd expect. Only people who eat them would know if they were delicious or not. They each have one of *those*, but you will never see *those* (children read this series too!).

Q **IS THERE A CHARACTER SETTING YOU ENDED UP CHANGING DRASTICALLY FOR *MERMAN IN MY TUB*? (MINAZOU)**

Drastically changed...I don't think so. But...when I couldn't decide, I showed my editor the current Hisatora and a handsome young Hisatora version. I was told to use the old man version. Wakasa hasn't changed much: I just wanted to depict "relationship" and "dependence." Er, I think so, anyway...

Q **HOW DO TAKASU AND THE OTHERS COME TO VISIT THE HOUSE? (SHOOTING STAR)**

From the river where Tatsumi picked up Wakasa, there is a secret underground sewer that they use to get to a manhole near the outside of the bathroom. His grandfather made it. (Don't think about the legal implications of that; this is a romance.) The ones who can walk easily dash over on land at night.

Q **I ALWAYS READ THIS WITH MY SEVENTH-GRADE DAUGHTER. THIS IS A BOLD QUESTION FROM A PARENT AND CHILD, BUT... HOW DO WAKASA AND THE OTHERS GO TO THE BATHROOM? (I FEEL LIKE WAKASA WOULD SAY, "I'M AN IDOL SO I DON'T GO TO THE BATHROOM~!" (LAUGH)) (HIPOPOTAMASU)**

Thank you for being parent and child fans! Bathroom...Well, now that you've used the "idols" excuse, I can't use it.
Oh, I know... I'm sure they all have abnormal bodies and use up everything they consume to give them health or prolong their longevity. Oh, but Kasumi doesn't go to the bathroom either! (｀･∀･´)

I WONDERED WHILE READING. DO THE CHARACTERS CUT THEIR HAIR WHEN IT GROWS TOO LONG? (KUROKANA)

It takes a really long time for it to grow so they just leave it as is, but if it gets too long they ask Takasu to cut it. Takasu is the only one who takes care of his hair regularly to prevent split ends.

 I TRIED TAKING A BATH WITH MY FEET TOGETHER LIKE WAKASA, BUT IT WAS SUPER HARD. I ALMOST FELL ON MY FACE. DOES WAKASA ALWAYS LIVE LIKE THIS? OR DOES HE HAVE TATSUMI HELP HIM MOST OF THE TIME? (PECORO)

G...Good job...! I've tried it too, but it made me get a leg cramp. However, Wakasa has always trained this way and has been a merman for a long time, so he is pretty okay. But outside of the manga, he gets a lot of help from Tatsumi. ☆ That's why Tatsumi always carries work gloves in his back pocket.

 WHEN TAKASU, MIKUNI-SAN, MAKI-SAN, AGARI-SAN, AND GOROMARU VISIT, DON'T TATSUMI'S NEIGHBORS FIND OUT? (BLUE SKY)

They come through a special route so that they don't get found out (see previous page). They all have skills to avoid humans so they are even safer!

 TATSUMI HAS A CUTE LITTLE SISTER LIKE KASUMI-CHAN, BUT DOES WAKASA HAVE ANY SIBLINGS? IT'S MY OWN IMAGINATION, BUT I FEEL LIKE WAKASA WOULD HAVE AN OLDER BROTHER!! (TARO)

Wakasa has no siblings or parents. But he played as a little brother to Takasu and the others, so they are like siblings! He looks up to Agari as a senpai because he wanted to be spoiled a little, too.

 DOES WAKASA HAVE A MAN'S OR WOMAN'S HEART? (G-LOVE)

A man's heart! He is a merman with a male body and soul that likes cute things a bit and is influenced by women's magazines!

 WHY IS TAKASU SO TANNED? (AYANO)

He's always busy in the water (or sea) or out on land. Just kidding, it's because he looks stronger and manlier when he's a little tan.

Itokichi
Wakasa
Umehara Yuuichirou
Tatsumi
Shimazaki Nobunaga
Takasu
Suzuki Tatsuhisa
Echizen
Yusa Kouji

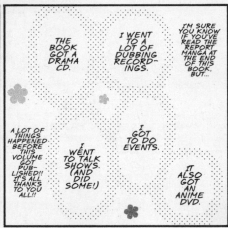

WHAT IF... SOUSUKE WAS THE MAIN CHARACTER?

Presented by ITOKICHI

HUMANIZED

AN "I WANT TO SEE THIS KIND OF ILLUSTRATION" REQUEST!

+VARIOUS JOBS

I THOUGHT THE "LIGHT HUMANIZED" WERE REALLY INTERESTING...!! IT FEELS STRANGE AND A BIT EMBARRASSING.